Central Air

Central Air

Mike Puican Poems

TRIQUARTERLY BOOKS/NORTHWESTERN UNIVERSITY PRESS

EVANSTON, ILLINOIS

TriQuarterly Books
Northwestern University Press
www.nupress.northwestern.edu

Copyright © 2020 by TriQuarterly Books/Northwestern University Press.
Published 2020. All rights reserved.

Printed in the United States of America

10   9   8   7   6   5   4   3   2   1

Library of Congress Cataloging-in-Publication Data
Names: Puican, Mike, author.
Title: Central air : poems / Mike Puican.
Description: Evanston : TriQuarterly Books/Northwestern University Press,2020.
Identifiers: LCCN 2020012479 | ISBN 9780810142077 (paperback) |
    ISBN9780810142084 (ebook)
Subjects: LCSH: Chicago (Ill.)—Poetry. | LCGFT: Poetry.
Classification: LCC PS3616.U378 C46 2020 | DDC 811.6—dc23
LC record available at https://lccn.loc.gov/2020012479

for Mary Hawley

CONTENTS

The Lawyer Says   *1*

***

And the Gauchos Sing   *5*

Red Line   *6*

Joke   *7*

Bill's Blues   *8*

Still Life with Pears   *9*

Tequila and Steve   *10*

Englewood in Bloom   *12*

Sudden Rain   *13*

Sunset at a Lake   *14*

Immigrant Grasses   *15*

Friday Night Poker   *17*

Man Digging a Sidewalk   *18*

Chicago   *19*

Unbridled   *21*

Clark and Belmont Ghazal   *22*

Vi Redd at the Clef Club   *23*

Central Air   *24*

Somniloquy   *29*

All-Night Delivery   *30*

Loved One   *31*

Abandoned Church   *32*

Psalm   *33*

When He's Dead   *34*

Poem with Many Endings   *35*

The Magi Ask for Directions   *36*

The Priest Was Either Discussing Death   *37*

Drying the Dishes   *38*

Subtle Is the Lord   *39*

Good News   *40*

Light in Hell   *41*

Fall   *43*

Settlement   *44*

Dating Again   *46*

Why I'm in Marketing   *47*

30 Seconds   *48*

Nonfiction   *49*

La Calle de los Salvados   *50*

Knife in the Wall   *52*

The Call   *53*

Abundance   *54*

We Are Part of a Story That Is Far from Ending   *56*

Eden Is Lost   *57*

Here   *59*

The Current   *60*

The Dusk   *61*

Saint Prisca   *62*

Acknowledgments   *63*

Notes   *67*

The Lawyer Says

"Show me a fireball of desire, a current
of wild horses, the unquenched thirst
of stone lions. Where's the evidence

that stars rise from watery graves,
that fish swim in the sleep
of schoolchildren?"

The judge checks her watch.
She thinks of her lover's body touched
by the morning's sun. She could use

a cigarette. Suddenly a lion enters
the courtroom. The lawyer's body
is lodged between the big cat's teeth.

Silence descends on the courtroom as he
disappears into the dark. "Fools," he cries.
"Your language! It's not dangerous enough!"

And the Gauchos Sing

for Barry Silesky

Catalpas blooming up and down Catalpa Street, car alarms blooming
up and down Waveland Avenue—an instant of nature without the narrative.
O face-in-your-morning-juice, swimmer-in-an-old-wool-suit,
we sit side by side on the steps smoking the same cigarette,
watching children who live alone, women married to the wrong men.

Here is your little dog roaming the alley. What will he do for love this time?
The gauchos sing, "The silver lights of stars hurl themselves
against the open pampas of Clark Street." O tomato-in-a-woman's-palm,
one millisecond following the next millisecond, "Heal thyself,"
the poem says, "Discard your beggar's mat and walk."

You hurl yourself into traffic. You talk to cops and street thugs;
they smile at their smartphones. They strut in the sun like jackals
after a kill. And the gauchos sing: "Everyone will finally leave you, fugitive."
A cloud of pigeons cuts through the smog. Everyone will finally leave you.

When the bus comes we sing like sailors. A red sky presses you to its lips.
I tell you that everything has already been written. You say
that on a long, difficult pilgrimage Bashō wrote on his hat.

Red Line

Knife slicing the living night,
nacreous river, we've stood waiting for you
many times before. And still we wait.

River of departure, arrival, departure.
Container of all ambition, you make us
what we are: employable, fuckable.

Night-blue finger tracing the lake's shore,
airstream of avarice and hearts askew,
carved into the suddenly valuable land

of broken-down homes and buried
children. Our hopes, our bodies fill you,
conductor, with metal cheeks,

200-watt eyes offering glimpses
of bedrooms, overstuffed chairs and
their punishments, storefronts

lit like flames. You carry day traders
dressed for sentencing, young mothers
working on resumes, outcasts

busking for change. In your care,
a steady ticking, the learned comfort of metal
on metal, the caress of night feathers.

O snake among the roses, we
await your approach, the cold snap
of your doors flung wide open.

Joke

The one Dad told, after Uncle Hank's homemade beer:
A dog walks into a bar and orders a beer.

As a child there were things I never mentioned:
dogs walking into bars, ordering beers,

Uncle Hank coming home drunk asking me to dance.
A dog walks into a bar and orders a beer.

In the '90s, I drank, smoked pot, shot pool while
dogs under the bar lapped our spilled beers.

"Put your head in this noose." And I do.
A dog walks into a bar and orders a beer.

Then custody battles over who gets the dog.
The dog waits at the bar nursing its beer.

Dog, my little flame, ignite this bar,
You, me, our beers.

Invented life: we can say anything!
A mallard walks into a bar and orders a duckquiri.

Once again, a bartender walks up to me and says:
"S'up, dog? Need a beer?"

Bill's Blues

The first time we sense that a pine tree really doesn't need us . . .
we feel alienated and depressed. The second time . . . we feel joyful.

—ROBERT BLY

But tonight I see that Little Ed
doesn't need me and the Blues

Imperials don't need me either. Bill
the owner, the two busboys making out

in the corner, the granite bar top:
none of them need me. The Red Bulls

and vodka, my wife's butt pushing
against me, the photo of the naked punker

on a plate of spaghetti hung above the bar:
none of them could give a shit.
                               Baby,
the busboys are doing shots and the band

is cranked, push your butt up against me
again. The red, blue, green spots, the pop

pop from the band, the bass player's
spiked hair, the kid who snuck in to sell

plastic roses to the crowd. When I reach
down to take one, it lights up.

Still Life with Pears

Past panhandlers and then the doorman,
a vision forms—part light, part Asian pears.
Shadows from the silk drapes sweep wetly,
kiln-dried chairs of the Belle Époque
bloom. A cloud of spring pollen drifts in and
settles on the mahogany lake of the
dining room table. Underneath it a child's mind
is flat black. Now his chin's perched on the rim of it.

The ghosts of immigrants who once lived
on this same ground say, "Pity this boy.
His heart knows only the cage of his own ribs."
My mother stirs currents of cookie dough.
She shudders as the sun ignites the buzzing stem
of a rose. She says to me, "Need more vase."

Tequila and Steve

After all the bars on Broadway
closed, they walked outside.

He was the Butter Man, also
known as Steve; she was

Susan but on weekends
went by Tequila. Above them

the sky reared, flame-
edged, over the firepit

called Chicago.
What time was it?

It was Saturday and the
heat had just begun to arrive.

As they walked, he felt
his heart sprint ahead.

She was the one
who asked the time

but the clock was them.
The sun ignited a marble bust

ringed by sugar maples,
a family pushing an *elote* cart

down the street, a tiny spider
dangling above her doorway.

In her kitchen, a pan
sizzled with oil while faint notes

rose from a piano downstairs.
The scents of fried eggs

and just-cut lilacs filled
the air while the back

of her neck and a can of beer
created a near-perfect tranquility.

Englewood in Bloom

He is a giant with the voice of a girl; he
sings. Englewood stands at the window
above the Apostolic Lighthouse Church,
dawn striating the avenue and all of its
regular and irregular red townhomes.
As with the young girls who ride giggling
up and down Front Street all night when they
should be home in bed—so it is with him:
"Work hard all your young days and find
yourself with your soul out among the
gray doves all night on a phone wire."

He is tired of April's smallness,
the little leaves. He thinks: Are those
snowbells or do I make them snowbells?
Are flowers little dreams of desire, like
the wallpaper designs repeating or
sidewalks made to expand and contract
with changes in temperature? A stockbroker
dances in the street. Someone's saxophone
describes the world. A cool breeze through
the open window lifts Englewood's shirt.
He sings.

Sudden Rain

As I write this, the snow melts; the landscape
regains its dignity. One by one

the streetlights spark and ignite.
A sudden rain becomes a layer of darkness

the world moves through. A darkness
not like one I've known.

The moon rises over an open field, soybeans
sprout in all directions, birds perch in trees,

grackles and skycatchers mostly,
their small beaks aimed for a few seconds

at Mars. In the distance a tangled string
of commuter traffic eventually

unties. There is contained in this moment
some possibility the last one did not have.

Step aside, Lord, step aside . . .

Sunset at a Lake

A woman sings to her daughter

in the grass; a teenager

      argues   with her boyfriend

on a cell phone; an air conditioner

            shudders

from a snack shop on the beach.

Three men watch two TVs in the shade.

Sweat bees circle

      their beer cans.   A five-year-old

squeals from the top of Sheridan's horse.

            The sun moves

in slow increments of dying.

A phone line cuts the sky like a

closed eye.

      Mars brightens   as dusk

twists its way into our hearts.

            A mosquito pulls

from my arm until full.

Immigrant Grasses

Words, overheard
in garden shops,
        uptown and earnest,
blossom into cablegrams

        from South Korea
or Cameroon; oleander,
        unscented blue star,
becomes

        a refugee
from a royal Malaysian family
        exhausted
from her long ocean voyage;

        gladioli, pale green
and unblossomed,
        in uncertain translation,
become voluminous

        and bloodred;
common yellow snapdragons
        conjure
the emblazoned railway

        embankments
of Bucharest.
        Radiant,
reassembled, worlds

        arise from colonnades
of cosmos,
        from nasturtium
and bloodroot

reshaped on someone's
far-traveled tongue:
        alyssum
of untold losses,

        immigrant grasses
rising between
        the floorboards.
Unsettled

        and urgent: images
created by
        gardeners
and railway conductors,

        shipbuilders and
fruit polishers,
        nurturers whose
worlds crest,

        broad-leafed
and crimsoned, whose words
        offer the chance
to grow fluent in

        something
that has no concern
        over what meanings
are indigenous.

        after "Nothing Stays Put" by Amy Clampitt

Friday Night Poker

Once, my father, his shit-hearted boss, and
our dick landlord stopped their late-night
poker game, gazed down at me lying

in my crib and melted in love. Now God,
in the same way, as he looks upon you,
me, and everyone in this broke-ass town,

melts in love. He can't help himself.
Is God on drugs? He needs to take a deep
breath and calm himself. But no!

He's changed the rules: the gates of hell
are closed! Souls, once condemned
for eternity, have been lifted up, each

carried like some saint into heaven! Look,
God now casts his indiscriminate light
upon this town and all the rest of heaven and

earth, and we become like babies, unjudged,
blameless, once again reflected in another's
wide-open eyes that hold us completely.

Man Digging a Sidewalk

Morning at a busy intersection,
under a large elm, a young man
with thick short arms digs up
a sidewalk. He works steadily,
at his own pace. I watch him
and the elm's leaves, turned yellow,
edged with brown. A teenager
walks past the young man and over
the mounds of dirt. She leads
her dog, a chihuahua dressed
as a honeybee. The morning's light
pours over the girl and her dog.
As they climb another mound
of dirt, the dog turns to me and says,
"Don't fuck with me. I'm capable
of anything. I am boundless."
These are the early days of autumn.
The mind soars, let our bodies
keep watch over the work.

Chicago

City of car alarms, a chair
        flying out a second story
                window—no one asks if

there's a story. Cigarettes
        in a doorway, congregation
                at Sunday service holier than thou

but not indifferent
        to the tangled cable
                of voices calling for change to be

now. A young mother
        carries a FIGHT
                FOR $15 sign. She has plans for more

than quilts on the floor or
        cardboard taped on broken
                windows, has hopes for more than

listening to
        city officials
                who hate

to lose explain why a teenaged boy
        was shot sixteen times. BLACK LIVES
                MATTER is seen on front lawns or

in apartment windows
        while protesters lock arms
                to stop traffic. An atmosphere

of sadness
        and outrage permeates
                the city. Let us step

alongside the dreams and desires
        of bricklayers, smelt fishers,
                patched-up families waiting in

line at Jewel, old women
        and men walking down
                the street in splendor,

electricians and store managers
        tossing back shots,
                shouting insults to mortify

those who ignore
        the sounds of el trains,
                furniture flying out windows, our

cacophonous voices
        rising until we free
                ourselves of these willful wolves.

        a Golden Shovel poem after "Gay Chaps at the Bar"
        by Gwendolyn Brooks

Unbridled

The fry cook, who is also a horse,
looks past the moving lips of the
commencement's bulwark against

moral encroachment for whom there's
great warmth among the graduates
and other hopefuls. The fry cook

takes a deep breath and shouts PUNK!
He saunters past the bleachers while
a missionary, who is also a horse,

talks about forced birth control and
civilized latrine practices. A team
of colts, who are also graduate students,

exchange tips on how to locate hotel
rooms rented by the hour. The fry cook
looks up to the sky and prays for rain.

Clark and Belmont Ghazal

Two window washers radio for help when the Sky Climber hits a scaffold
on the way down. Someone yells out: Raise it the fuck up!

Three brothers turn on every faucet in the church bathroom then
sprint for the door. They push each other into bushes all the way home.

A woman applies her makeup at a traffic light while a chanteuse
pours her heart through a crack in the window.

An old man walks his wiener dog—her swayed back, nails clicking,
nipples just off the sidewalk—connecting the neighborhood.

"People," says a waitress standing on the counter, "are we letting perfect
be the enemy of good?" A plane flies in her left ear and out her cheek.

Commuters on the platform eat spiced meat and fries while
leaning against the heads of men who say they will cut our taxes.

We stand in silence, facing the same direction, waiting
for the next train, thinking we're not moving.

Vi Redd at the Clef Club

A crash like broken leaded glass
                from percussion
        beyond the generally understood world.

Vi responds with sax
                depositing unsafe ideas
        into Miss Betty Carter's change purse.

She leans into frantic Bird chords before
                a single long-held note
        injects starter fluid

into the crowd's fireless heart.
                Strutting past 2 A.M.
        and the manager's

repeated signals to stop, she
                breaks into *Now's the time!*
      Now's the time to wail!

Central Air

1. Car Troubles

Beyond the trash fires and the car burning serious oil
remained her strong reserve, which he mistook for options.

The dipstick nearly clean with ten blocks to go,
both of them married, looking for weed and unwilling

to call AAA as the night unraveled around some muddy
back alley's chain-link fence. Pounded by a rainstorm,

they stared at the thin red streaks from security cameras
and the unblinking stares of Rottweiler guard dogs

that seemed to say, "Go ahead, step out of the car."
A year later, in his studio apartment, he eats alone.

He still thinks they could have found a way out.

2. Tryst

Toddlers twirl across the dance floor
as the two sneak out the side exit. He's

in a chartreuse tie spilling down a blue-
hued shirt selected for the uncertain audition

of paladin to the paramour at the O'Hare Marriott.
Improvising by the pool, they splash

their hastily-tossed-across-the-lounge-chair jackets,
then chicken dance on the deck (sometimes touching).

His seersucker suit pants are soaking wet
as is her crimson brocade skirt.

Now they slip into her hotel room. Sunlight
falls on a street in Paris (or on a bed in Chicago).

An hour ago, laughing in line at the bar, they abruptly
skipped out (Back in a minute!) into the blurred future

with its appetite for color as red, green, and blue
bleed into the beige hotel room carpet.

3. Northside Bible Church of Abundant Love Picnic

Pigeons preen on wires backlit
by an evening sun, franks on the grill,
a young man from Romania trying to court
(could also be *transport* in Romanian)
the aloof girl at the church picnic. Once again,
he considers what little he knows about love;
he wonders if oak, willow, and olive
could somehow be translated into
what he understands as *oak*, *willow*,
and *olive*, which he also hopes might be
an example of that notion of revelation
he's heard so much about.

4. *Graduation*

After eight straight semesters
of classes packed with high achievers,
she stands in line at the club.

Warm breezes stir the streets as she
watches the smear of smiling families
on the sides of passing buses.

She's struck by the peal and echo of
dance music and the unexpected gentleness
of guards checking everyone's handbags.

Tonight, she didn't bring a handbag.
She steps into the pulsing music and lights;
she can't wait to see what happens.

First this happens, then this happens.
In a large swath of wakefulness,
she stares at his bedroom ceiling as

fish swim upstream along a riverbank
alive with midsummer color. She hears
notes of a piano her mother played

rise into the night. Outside lies the
city, as familiar as her favorite purse,
which tonight she left behind,

bringing only enough for admission
to the club, a drink, and cab fare home
tucked into the pocket of her jeans.

5. *Domestic Disturbance*

The air conditioner rumbles
under the broken windows
facing the back-alley stairs.

Carefully she steps around the glass
as she considers all the compromises
her mother would call

                "making it work,"

which

       she describes to the policewoman,
then over the phone to the social worker,
then, as accurately as possible, to herself, as

she stands a few yards from the man
shouting from the back seat of the squad car
asking her,

          once again, to forgive everything.

Somniloquy

Each morning my father disappeared like the moon,
then returned in time for prayers before bed.

The soul reaches towards its wildness. Doubting
Thomas's hand reaches toward his savior's wound.

Here is the priest rubbing oil into my forehead.
Now he blesses me: priest, prophet, and king.

Now I am five and sitting in dirt. Now
I'm in the kitchen taking apart the toaster.

Then one day I ask myself: Am I really the change—
driving twenty miles each weekday before dawn?

I hear choirs of angels sing as the elevator opens
to my father's nursing care floor.

Here is my dad teaching me to change a water pump.
He holds the water pump; I tighten the bolts.

The first chill of winter fills the garage. Yesterday,
I used a sawzall to open a wall. I worked slowly

so nails didn't pop through the drywall. Today
at my window, I watch believers file into Sunday Mass.

I watch the snow fall straight down in this rented room.
When I wake he holds me.

All-Night Delivery

Everybody dies—as though that fucked, I mean fact,
brings us closer to being understood

and forgiven. Tonight freezing winds blow through
our hosiery. Bands of ankles sing—their songs

are beautiful and intact for some, shattered for others.
At this late hour everyone is still awake: the cop

arriving home after working two shifts;
the baby who's been alternately crying and giggling

for the past eighteen hours, the pizza delivery guy exiting
the driveway of the drug addicts who, after two days,

are still jamming to music. Just as you and I sit
on the couch listening as the dust mites in the cushions

say to us: *Dear hearts, you have so many, many nights
ahead of you, and this one may never end.*

Loved One

The graveyard beyond a black window.
I'm already on the other side of the window
listening to the landscape and all its implications:
this tree and that shrub.
I rub a broken snail shell between my fingers.

Here at the town's edge
a blue jay settles on the nervous surface of the dead.
Something like water ticks; rotting leaves in a thinned creek.
Death's music rises.
The trees guide my slide into dark.

The linden says to me, "You're not as strong
as you think. Close your eyes. Change your mind."

Let there be a God that sees this.
Then a light, a grieving, a swatch of childhood,
let there be a father, an affection that suffices.
Let there be a memory that finally,
irrevocably resolves; even as it is also capitulation.
Let there be someone who sees this.

Abandoned Church

Caved-in church, colorless side-hill cemetery,
always present smell of the pulp mill
in the distance: an early August heat is rising
and that might be dew all over your body.

A creek trickles and ticks past the graves.
A fallen tree lies in the mud. You step over it,
leaving tracks, leaving the gray dawn
flapping its ghost wings.

So intense is your listening you wonder
if it's God's voice and all that is joined to it—
weed-surge and bee swarm: a small, insistent voice,
barely audible, almost a song. Let it speak.

You lean against the stone church wall, light
the day's first cigarette, and listen to a restless
southwest wind that leaves nothing alone.
Not God's voice. But whose?

Psalm

Your tape gun and trowel set the rules
for their observation, as do the drop cloths, the
        tuna and cheese in your lunch box,
the hard rain mixed with mulberries

        beating on the front door. Outside
the clouds are a spectrum of gray above the rows
        of black oak. You rest. The room
brightens with a crack of sunlight.

        Now you are thinking
of the coneflowers lying in the garbage—
        a layer of drywall, a layer
of coneflowers. They call out:

        Speak, Lord, that we know
the wind and rain, the rushing
        water and fragrant grasses.
The refrain allows the mind to rest; the body

        interprets that as joy.
You sit while the still wet walls dry. Outside,
        there are two seasons: summer,
and the one called summer.

When He's Dead

He can finally stop wondering whether God exists
or why he never had the nerve to hug his father.
He no longer has to say, "A part of me
feels uncomfortable with the Democrats." Finally,
he can stop thinking of what he should have said
at the custody hearing, how he shouldn't have been
so flip to the court-ordered psychologist.
He can stop daydreaming about the tree of heaven
that grows fifteen feet each year even though
the Polish lady cuts it to the ground each spring.
He can stop composing what he would say to the daughter
he hasn't seen in seventeen years, stop trying to catch
the cat on the counter licking the margarine,
stop worrying about the dreams in which he has
sex with the local crossing guard. No longer
will he have to wait in a barely moving line
at the city auto pound at two in the morning reading
a new-age pamphlet that says everything is good
and will be getting even better very soon.

Poem with Many Endings

Every day Raúl sent out for coffee, every day
he told me about his life on the south side.

Every night the moon said: *I am not the one
of whom you sing. Save your voice. Stand in my light.*

I dreamt Raúl and I walked through the surf holding our robes up,
the scents of melon and clove leading us to heaven.

Sometimes the two of us would sit for hours in silence. Sometimes
the heart attempts to weed an entire forest.

Hidden edge of the room, unfathomable curse.
Entire lifetimes are spent preparing for other lifetimes.

I take my pills. I lie on the Afghan rug half-dressed in light.
"Relax," Raúl says, "it becomes a story only after it's over."

The Magi Ask for Directions

Turn right at the Olive Garden
then follow the resurrection

of the dead past all that is seen and
unseen. Take the communion

of saints for about thirty minutes,
eventually it'll become two lanes.

Pass the boarded-up Bethlehem
Steel plant, the true God, worshipped

and glorified, in the distance you'll
see a Target. Follow signs for

another mile or two. You can't miss it.
It's just beyond the Land's End.

The Priest Was Either Discussing Death

after "Appendix C" by Anne Carson

The priest was either discussing death or he was not.

If he was discussing death, the listener was either visibly moved or was unaffected.

If she was unaffected, either his words were not understood or she was not in church at the time.

If she was not in church, she either went to an earlier Mass or lied about going to church.

If she went to an earlier Mass, either she told the priest she liked the sermon or was distracted from the sermon because there were too many valves open in her heart.

If she was distracted from the sermon because there were too many valves open in her heart, it was caused either by sunlight through the stained-glass window or the limits of form.

If it was the limits of form, the natural world was enjoying a moment of strength. Either that

or she had been considering the uncertainty between a hand and what's recalled as touch.

Or maybe it wasn't a hand and touch at all. Maybe it was the black of a closed mouth, or an open one, caught in the pattern, the pattern of no longer returned human love.

Drying the Dishes

My mother, who is washing the dishes,
places another plate in the drying rack. It's still dirty.
She says, "When you are done drying, you can rest.
Both of us can rest."

My father, who is also dead, sits in a chair,
newspapers and clothes strewn across the floor.
He puts his hand on my arm and says,
"Let's not get up today."

Subtle Is the Lord

In the Realm of the Five Senses what does desire attach to?
The wildness of the heart increases in the dark.
The absence of God only makes it wilder.
Wearing bird suits we lie in our beds. We sing.

The wildness of the heart increases in the dark.
You say, "Subtle is the Lord; my head is tied to a pole."
You lie in your bed in a bird suit. You sing
a song not so much unsung as wordless.

Subtle is the Lord; your head is tied to a pole.
You say, "For God to speak, remove your hands from His throat."
A song not so much unsung as wordless
and soundless—in broken glass, rainwater, traces of light.

For God to speak, remove whose hands from His throat?
In the Realm of the Five Senses, what does desire attach to:
broken glass, pools of rainwater, this faint light?
You say, "The presence of God only makes it wilder."

Good News

Mom pretends to be cleaning behind the couch.
Dad's in the basement trying to figure which
pipes lead upstairs. Black suit on a hot summer day,
the young man stands in our doorway
as though there are souls to be saved.

Grandpa doesn't care about answers, he's happy
for the company. *How do you know it's true?*
A tree crushed the minivan, the basement's
been flooded for days and Grandpa wants a sign.
I'm taillights the second I get my driver's license.

Dad swears through the floor. Hitting the pipes
doesn't help but sometimes it's the only solution.
The visitor points to his book. *Directions
are available.* He watches my sister
dance barefoot in the next room.

Jesus said that proof is all around us. A refugee
lifts his son from a car, ties his dog to a meter,
and delivers groceries; a ten-year-old
pushes on the chest of a man collapsed in a doorway.
Could this have happened by accident?

As I crank the stereo louder, he turns to me:
Have you been asked the Golden Question?
I tell him we've got to get out of this place.
He stares back at me, his fingers drum
along the spine of the prayer book.

Light in Hell

An ice-slicked rush hour skids down
your throat as you enter the on-ramp.
Eventually you slide into a driveway,
or the idea of a driveway,

or the idea of a domestic life. Later
the cat will sit on your head for hours.
Your husband will look into its eyes and
say how much you've disappointed him.

Dread leaps from the bedroom window.
The cat drags something barely alive
through the house. Your husband drains
the oil from your Subaru. You say to me,

Yes, this small room in which you
and I are drinking will do nicely.

Moonlight illuminates the iced branches.
Inside, your body also brightens in light—
incandescent light, flashlight, refrigerator
light, fluorescent light, candlelight.

Shadows cut into the room as your relatives
appear in the doorway: *Dear, have you tried
hard enough? You need to be willing to sacrifice
to make a relationship work.*

But hopelessness is a room of terrible
translation. Instead you hear: *You can
leave this dogpile of darkness, this
wicked streak in hell, this marriage.*

Yes, this small room in which you and I
are drinking will do nicely.

Fall

after "Spring" by Gerald Stern

The dawn, the dawn after a nightlong rain.
The poem, the one by Gerry Stern. The alley,
the alley I turn down as falling leaves loosen
the brightly painted girl of the waterfall
within me about whom I've kept silent for decades.
The linden, the linden slowly dying that
later will return alive and Eros standing naked
among the parked cars. What does he want of me,
shameless, unraveling the threadlike thing
woven from the bright intersections of avenues,
the touch that speaks both cherishing and farewell?
I watch a jet float through an el train. I slip
past the rush hour as quietly as an old man
coming home for supper. Where is my narrative?
A chorus of locusts cries out; a woman with
red shoes and pocketbook spins; the streets
intersecting Clark Street scatter and disentangle.

Settlement

There's a way men talk about weather,
what causes nails to back out,
when the lake's ready to drive on,
how someone once hauled a house over the ice
and was never heard from again.

Dad and I couldn't keep a straight face
at the luncheon on negotiations.
*"Creating options requires that you think
of things not already in your head."*
I laughed till milk came out my nose.

I'd watch him in a tree with a chainsaw,
huge branches dropping on the road.
Once we stopped at a corner restaurant
and there was a jazz band that made me cry.
We sang Hidey Hidey Ho with everyone else.

We would spend hours with our faces
inches apart fixing a sink, installing
a ceiling fan. He believed a person's story
was told in their work, that it's important
to tell that story so as to not be held by it.

Most days my story's told in dollar signs.
I shake hands, smile, lie, and have lunch.
Then am lied straight back to. Each meeting
ending with something faxed to lawyers.
There was a time he and I sat at lunch with smudges

of ash on our foreheads. We ate tomato soup
and grilled cheese sandwiches. Now
he visits me in the city. Performance artists
throw zucchinis at us from the stage.
We applaud because that is what we do next.

Dating Again

The DJ on the radio says witches are on the brink
or something like that. Wild horses cross the highway in ones
and twos. A shirtless man waves to me from the median strip.

A siren pierces the air. As I pull over, a bird screams.
The scent of burnt houses blows in through my air vents.
A cop shines a light in my face and I have ten seconds

to decide: give up the next three-to-five years
of my life or step on the gas and keep that sweet edge
I left the dance with before all the shooting started.

Why I'm in Marketing

A boy helps his uncle install a bathtub. Aunt Jillian was so pleased.
Now he owns a plumbing supply store. One kind word and we're

ophthalmologists. How does this happen? When I was seventeen
I told my dad I'd never sell out. Now I wake up surrounded

by positioning statements. It's our chance to be somebody—
the clerk typist who sees into the future, the head of Accounting

who hums at the urinal, the VP who flirts in the mailroom.
The founder started this from nothing. He could sell anything

to anybody. He taught his parakeet to say the company tagline.
The guy from HR says, "Money's the third reason people work."

Is it the health plan? The free samples of product? What she's
crossing and uncrossing as I explain why sales are down?

The three-story woman in a negligee was my idea. It stopped
traffic but no one bought the oatmeal. Now Security wants

to escort me to my office. They tell me to bring some empty boxes.
The founder bursts into the room, "We're not selling breakfast,

we're selling escape." Everyone pretends to write it down.
The parakeet sticks its head through the bars, it can't

get it back in. The clerk typist gazes into her crystal
and says, "This is starting to piss me off."

30 Seconds

It doesn't have to make sense; it just has to
sell product. *You are not the same person
you used to be. Why use the same shampoo?*

The actress practices her lines as someone applies
her makeup. Down the street a woman put
stones in her pockets and drowned.

Dryer sheets become spring rain, ready-to-bake
desserts are cookies in the oven at Grandma's,
floor cleaners: pine forests. Over time the lines

dissolve. Voices blur to a steady hum: a couple
argues in a doorway; a funeral procession
turns the corner singing "Amazing Grace."

The focus group said: too much lather, not enough
conditioning. It's not what they expected.
You start with a clear line of action. It becomes a story

but not the one you want. We let the mourners pass,
then return to the shoot. Bring in more lights,
we're losing the sun. Someone cue the pigeons.

Nonfiction

She was no Marilyn. He
was not uninterested.

There was no sliver of moon
whose light made inside
the same as outside.

She had little to lose; he hadn't
come here to talk.

This was no time to lose the keys.

If today had been Tuesday,
if the limo driver had spoken English . . .

No, she did not want a back rub.

Or was it silver blooming
against the night's sky?

But she didn't mind him looking.

Glass from the car window
exploded into a boundless night.

Those were not cries for help.

La Calle de los Salvados

At a stoplight, Celia Cruz sings:
I am but a wind-tossed leaf longing

for her lover's touch. A messenger
waits on his bike beside a woman

in a convertible around whom
the bolero rises. No one in this traffic

would be surprised to see the sun
darkened by this woman's tear-

streaked face, to see her smudged
blue eyelids make disappear

the clear, widening sky. Two dozen
schoolchildren walk through her tears.

They carry flowers from a garden
her heart has trampled through.

The messenger's hands are golden;
they're pollen covered, just as

her red leather seats and matching purse
are pollen covered. As she waits,

the entire third grade floats past her car.
She thinks: Why have I cried so long?

The light turns green and two sounds
break loose: the beating wings

of a cell phone in her handbag
and a street-fair tuba played by

a black bear announcing spring.

Knife in the Wall

Add to the clenched fist, the ex-convict
with his shirt off strumming an acoustic guitar.
Add to the three brothers and their dreams

of graffiti tags, rusted car parts and roses
tattooed on the bottoms of their feet. Add to the
house music rising from traffic, two boys tied

to a water heater while their mother smokes
a cigarette in a doorway. Add to the priest's
platitudes, the woman who after weeks of weeping

realizes she's hungry. Add to the knife in the wall,
the short man who stuck it there as he said
something to the boy to calm him. Add

nothing to the deathless wine that flows from
the short man's heart and is inexhaustible.

The Call

Mars flares above a frozen lake.
A jet's trail lines the sky like a closed eye.
A young boy straightens thick, fat fingers
to show what he is to become: five.
Another in a bright yellow jacket walks
across the ice—someone calls him back
from beyond the breakwater . . .

This evening my father appears
in the melting snow of a cornfield. I see him
now blooming from my face. A red fox
crosses the mud; a crack bursts from the ice.
Something puts its hands over my ears and says,
I am late May burning through Manitoba.
I am a bonfire blazing in the cold fog. Something
puts its hands over my ears and says, *Listen* . . .

Abundance

for Mary

This trembling, electrified,
off-phase abundance,

these broken amens,
misguided loves,

streets purged,
fire-bent, unquenched.

Here among the
neophytes and novices

are you, M, thirsty!
for experience,

for your chance to sing
"Too Hot to Handle"

out loud on the bus
ride home. Here is

your old Romanian poet,
uncertain songbird,

stale cornbread
minus 4%. The markets

crash, the funds collapse,
and still the beast

adores you; the beast
has always adored you.

My mind searches
for miracles—but

the miracles shift, they
scamper away like

salamanders in the sun,
they fall apart then

reassemble themselves
in your arms.

Ancient home, ancient
tree colors blazing

through north Chicago.
M, are you listening?

M, reach into the future.
No ambiguity, no

suffering need be lost
here in this waiting place—

in this capsized boat
painted with roses.

Pull me into
the future. Then and

then.

We Are Part of a Story That Is Far from Ending

An ash-black and ash-white evening. Gradually
thinning clouds hang in this rush hour traffic.
In another city my daughter draws pictures of trees
on fire. The letters I send are returned, unopened.
I let a car cut in from the slow lane.
His bumper sticker says: ACCOMMODATION ≠ HAPPINESS.
Grief grinds its cigarette out on my windshield.

There is a language of place, of setting,
spoken in the hard edges of traffic and said
only in gestures—wordless, articulate.
The couple across the street says goodbye
in a doorway. The arms of a boy on a park bench
disappear into his coat. A woman rests her head
against a streetlamp, then raises it and walks off.

In the city I left, I slept in the doorway
of the tenement that was torn down for the high-rise
I landed my first job in. Down the street
I was promoted, divorced, obtained the papers
for my visa. These places have as little meaning
as the piece of paper I'm writing on. Yet they mark
what's been kept, what's been left behind.

Tonight the crack in the asphalt is speaking to me,
the sparrow with moss tangled on its left foot.
Two families in a driveway talk between their cars
as the darkness gathers and spreads. No one
is making a move to leave. One by one,
I watch the vapor lamps down the street
spark and ignite. Love sees what the eyes see.

Eden Is Lost

Eden is lost,
but the kitchen

is here. It marks
the end of

our sadness. The rest:
God's pessimism.

This could be a bar
in Bucktown

where bartenders
labor in poverty

but not despair. See,
one lays her

head on the rail
as if on a threshold.

Outside, a dog
snarls at a mole,

shadows
began to take us leaf

by leaf. Two boys
with sticks

enact scenes of
war and death.

Beyond them
a rose shines

like a light. Today,
as I stack

the winter wood,
pine sap stains

articulate the moment.
Today, the soul

leaves the body. Finally
some work gets done.

Here

Here is our cat lapping its milk: fat cat, red tongue, green
mind and August, the unruliest month. The wildness of
the season: isn't that what you always wanted—the soul
glimpsing, the loss of privacy while playing the instrument,
the freedom without leaving the cage? You and I remain
"on vacation" while the government finds itself obliged
to react in "self-defense." The year is 2003, I mean 2018.
It's not who controls the production of goods as I thought.
The demagogue is doing the best he can; the *capitaine*
of industry is doing the best she can; God in heaven,
silent as it is, is doing the best it can. Fifteen years ago
you stood at the edge of Chicago, head cocked like a crow
eyeing a bag of garbage, broken and overflowing. You were
young and thought you knew nothing: you left blanks
for what you did not yet know. Today you and I write
at our desks while others take our places on earth. We
have this "accessibility" to experience, to the dead silence while
in Purgatory. We leave blanks for what we do not yet know.

The Current

after "Fermata" by Andrew Zawacki

One of me replays what he should have said
to the judge at the custody hearing. One of me
walks the shoulder of I-80 while the sumac
bursts into a scatter of sparrows. One of me wades
into a rain-filled rock quarry while another
me watches from the other side.

One's stomach knots up when his boss
enters the conference room. One's not sure
what a C-clamp is but he doesn't want to return
to his father without it. One checks his phone
two minutes after the last time he checked his phone.
One sleeps in an open field under a nickel sky.

Sitting on a bench in early spring, one
gets an erection. He's more surprised than anyone.
One of me throws his wallet into the street and
hitchhikes to Denver. He undresses the woman
he will marry in two years; he watches as she
steps into the shower. One stands on a bluff

as his parents' ashes sift through the trees below.
One says, "I'm stoned . . . I mean, starved."
He lets go of his father's hand, then sprints
into Main Street. One of me wonders
how a particular fire came to rest in his heart.
He checks his phone. He loves that color on her.

The Dusk

Moon, quarter moon, scents of sassafras
and lilac, leaves drained of all color.

Wind in the accumulating dusk shaking the white lilies,
the stands of late daylilies.

A swarm of gnats clouds one's vision.
What secret combustible makes a man quieter, more

polite? The day grinds to darkness.
It says something one does not want brought to mind.

Speak, Lord, I will forgive everything.

Saint Prisca

Young Christian martyr who was thrown to a lion at the amphitheater,
but the lion lay down at her feet. Later she was beheaded.

How does this happen: a lion next to me
licking my feet? Nothing occurs against God's will.
This lion cannot be anything but what it is,

starved and beaten. Nor can these spectators
do other than see through their eyes of boredom
and privilege. I look up at their faces and see

the face of the Lord. I sense Him in the silence
accumulating as they chant for my death.
This lion could turn into an emerald; the faces

in the stadium, peach blossoms; my feet,
sweet cream. Even as this is God's hand,
it is not a miracle. I have the deepest

sadness these spectators should lack the joy
the lion and I have. Each week a child is lowered
into the pit; each week the crowd throws kisses

to the lions. Their eyes are wide as if anticipating
the presence of the Lord. Today the lion and I
sit next to each other. We cannot do otherwise.

Just as the executioner who will soon
sever my head from my body cannot do otherwise.
All of us who do God's work.

ACKNOWLEDGMENTS

In gratitude: to Barry Silesky who, in twenty years of poetry workshops at his dining room table, taught me to write poetry. To Poetry Slam inventor Marc Smith, who gave me my first opportunities to write and perform poetry, and whose mentorship taught me that the audience comes first. To Parneshia Jones, who went above and beyond the requirements of any editor to help shape this book into one I am immensely proud of. To my good friend Mark Turcotte for his uncompromising commitment to artistic quality, his deep loyalty to his students, family, and friends, and his eye for the perfect cover. To C. Dale Young for being a tough and generous teacher, who pushed me to take risks and go deeper in my writing. To Reginald Gibbons for his generous, unwavering support for my writing as a workshop instructor, editor of my first chapbook, and shaper of the manuscript that became this book. To my first reader, fellow writer, and partner Mary Hawley for her high standards and expectations for my writing, and for the profound love, intimacy, and support she brings into my life every day.

To those who over many years have shaped, inspired, and supported me: Lucy Anderton, Bill Ayers, Dwayne Betts, Tara Betts, Nora Brooks Blakely, Rosellen Brown, Gabrielle Calvocoressi, Bob Chicoine, Tony Fitzpatrick, Regie Gibson, Gregorio Gomez, Ray González, Chris Green, Jennifer Grotz, Ralph Hamilton, Julia Haw, Larry Janowski, Tyehimba Jess, Allison Joseph, Jim Kagafas, Quraysh Ali Lansana, Miguel López Lemus, Haki Madhubuti, Simone Muench, Joseph Parisi, Coya Paz, Martha Rhodes, Ed Roberson, Jacob Saenz, Maureen Seaton, Alan Shapiro, Patricia Smith, Ann Stanford, Bridgette Turner, Luis Humberto Valadez, Ellen Bryant Voigt, Ellen Placey Wadey, Michael Warr, Eleanor Wilner, avery r. young, Steve Young

To the large community of friends, activists, and artists who accompany each other on a journey with no roadmap as we, in our individual ways, create beauty.

The author also thanks the editors of the following publications, in which poems in this collection, some in earlier versions, have previously appeared:

After Hours: "The Dusk," "The Magi Ask for Directions," "Sudden Rain," "Tequila and Steve"

Another Chicago Magazine: "Poem with Many Endings"

Blossom Bone: "This Morning, My Father" (an earlier version of "Sudden Rain")

Chicago Reader: Somniloquy

The Collagist: "The Current"

The Cortland Review: "The Call," "When He's Dead"

Hypertext: "Immigrant Grasses," Sunset at a Lake," "Red Line"

Jet Fuel Review: "Eden Is Lost," "Joke"

Linden Avenue: "Chicago"

The Literary Bohemian: "La Calle de los Salvados"

The Malahat Review: "Good News"

New England Review: "Psalm," "As If Talking" (an earlier version of "Sudden Rain"

Poetry: "And the Gauchos Sing"

Prick of the Spindle: "The Priest Was Either Discussing Death"

qarrtsiluni: "Fall"

RHINO: "Drying the Dishes"

Spoon River Poetry Review: "Man Digging a Sidewalk"

Third Coast Magazine: "Saint Prisca"

TriQuarterly: "The Lawyer Says," "Subtle Is the Lord"

"Englewood in Bloom" was included in the anthology *New Poetry from the Midwest 2014*, published by New American Press, 2014.

"Golden Shovel for Chicago" (now titled "Chicago") was included in *The Golden Shovel Anthology: New Poems Honoring Gwendolyn Brooks*, published by the University of Arkansas Press, 2017.

"Knife in the Wall" was included in the anthology *Revise the Psalm: Work Celebrating the Writing of Gwendolyn Brooks*, published by Curbside Splendor, 2017.

"Abundance" uses a version of a line from "OK Jazz Funeral Services" by William Fuller. "Englewood in Bloom" uses a version of a line from "The Sea-Elephant" by William Carlos Williams. "Immigrant Grasses" uses some images and language from "Nothing Stays Put" by Amy Clampitt. "Knife in the Wall" uses a version of a line from "Possibility: An Assay" by Jane Hirshfield. "Psalm" uses a version of a line from "The Smell of Death" by Gerald Stern. "Settlement" uses a version of a line from "10. FAMILY/ Grove" by Albert Goldbarth. "Sudden Rain" uses a version of a line from "Ode: at a twenty-four-hour gas station" by Reginald Gibbons. "Tequila and Steve" uses a version of a line from P-L-A-I-N-S by Paul Hoover.